M000197819

Earn. Save. Give.
Leader Guide

Earn. Save. Give.
Wesley's Simple Rules for Money

Earn. Save. Give.
978-1-63088-392-8
978-1-63088-393-5   eBook

Earn. Save. Give. - Large Print Edition
978-1-63088-394-2

Earn. Save. Give. - Leader Guide
978-1-63088-395-9
978-1-63088-396-6   eBook

Earn. Save. Give. - DVD
978-1-63088-397-3

Earn. Save. Give. - Program Guide
978-1-63088-398-0   Flash Drive
978-1-63088-399-7   Download

Earn. Save. Give. - Youth Study Book
978-1-63088-400-0
978-1-63088-401-7   eBook

Earn. Save. Give. - Children's Leader Guide
978-1-63088-402-4

Earn. Save. Give. - Devotional Readings for Home
978-1-5018-0507-3
978-1-5018-0509-7   Package of 25
978-1-5018-0508-0   eBook

For more information, visit www.AbingdonPress.com.

Also by James A. Harnish

A Disciple's Heart

A Disciple's Path

Believe in Me

Converge Bible Studies:
Women of the Bible

Journey to the Center of the Faith

Living with the Mind of Christ

Passion, Power, and Praise

Radical Renovation

reConnect

Rejoicing in Hope

Simple Rules for Money

Strength for the Broken Places

You Only Have to Die

JAMES A. HARNISH

Wesley's Simple Rules
for Money

Leader Guide

by Barbara Dick

Abingdon Press / Nashville

Earn. Save. Give.
Wesley's Simple Rules for Money

Leader Guide
by Barbara Dick

Copyright © 2015 Abingdon Press
All rights reserved.

No part of this work may be reproduced or transmitted in any form or by any means, electronic or mechanical, including photocopying and recording, or by any information storage or retrieval system, except as may be expressly permitted by the 1976 Copyright Act or in writing from the publisher. Requests for permission can be addressed to Permissions, The United Methodist Publishing House, P.O. Box 280988, 2222 Rosa L. Parks Boulevard, Nashville, TN 37228-0988, or e-mailed to permissions@umpublishing.org.

This book is printed on elemental, chlorine-free paper.
ISBN 978-1-63088-395-9

Scripture quotations unless noted otherwise are from the Common English Bible. Copyright © 2011 by the Common English Bible. All rights reserved. Used by permission. www.CommonEnglishBible.com.

Scripture quotations marked NRSV are taken from the New Revised Standard Version of the Bible, copyright 1989, Division of Christian Education of the National Council of the Churches of Christ in the United States of America. Used by permission. All rights reserved.

Scripture quotation marked (NIV) is taken from the Holy Bible, New International Version®, NIV®. Copyright © 1973, 1978, 1984, 2011 by Biblica, Inc.™ Used by permission of Zondervan. All rights reserved worldwide. www.zondervan.com. The NIV" and "New International Version" are trademarks registered in the United States Patent and Trademark Office by Biblica, Inc.™

Scripture quotation marked *The Message* is from *THE MESSAGE.* Copyright © by Eugene H. Peterson 1993, 1994, 1995, 1996, 2000, 2001, 2002. Used by permission of NavPress Publishing Group.

Scripture quotation marked *Good News* is from the Good News Translation in Today's English Version- Second Edition © 1992 by American Bible Society. Used by Permission.

The *Money Autobiography*, created by the Rev. Dan R. Dick, assistant to the bishop in the Wisconsin Annual Conference, is available at http://doroteos2.com/2015/02/11/money-autobiography/. The questions are used here by permission.

15 16 17 18 19 20 21 22 23 24— 10 9 8 7 6 5 4 3 2 1
MANUFACTURED IN THE UNITED STATES OF AMERICA

Contents

To the Leader

Welcome! In this study, you have the opportunity to help a group of learners examine the relationship between money and wisdom and its impact on our life of faith. Through the biblical witness and the teachings of John Wesley, James A. Harnish takes us on a journey of discovery and understanding that will lead to more faithful and fulfilled living.

It is often difficult to talk about money in the church. Our culture tells us that our relationship with and use of money is a private affair, nobody's business but our own. Engaging in open conversation about money may make some participants uncomfortable. Consider how to create the kind of safe learning environment in which they can share their experiences and feelings honestly, as well as listen with sensitivity to others.

Scripture tells us that where two or three are gathered together, we also will find the Holy Spirit, working in and through all those gathered. As you prepare to lead, pray for that presence and expect that you will experience it.

This four-session study includes use of the following components:

- the book *Earn. Save. Give.: Wesley's Simple Rules for Money*, by James A. Harnish;
- this Leader Guide;
- the video segments that accompany the study.

Participants in the study will also need Bibles, as well as either a spiral-bound notebook for a journal or an electronic means of journaling, such as a tablet. If possible, notify those who may be interested in the study in advance of the first session. Make arrangements for those participants to get copies of the book so that they can read the Introduction and Chapter 1.

Using This Guide With Your Group

Because no two groups are alike, this guide has been designed to give you flexibility and choice in tailoring the sessions for your group. The session format is listed below. You may choose any or all of the activities shown, adapting them as you wish to meet the schedule and needs of your particular group.

Most group sessions won't be long enough to do all the activities. Select ahead of time which activities the group will do, for how long, and in what order. In some sessions, video clips or music selections are suggested. While these resources can give participants a multisensory experience, they are not essential to the study. Depending on which activities you select, there may be special preparation needed. The leader is alerted to what is needed up front in the session plan.

Session Format

Planning the Session
    Session Goals
    Biblical Foundation
    Special Preparation

Getting Started
Welcome
Opening Prayer
Opening Activities

Learning Together
Video Study and Discussion
Bible Study and Discussion
Book Study and Discussion

Wrapping Up
Closing Activity
Closing Prayer

Helpful Hints

Preparing for the Sessions

- Pray for the leading of the Holy Spirit as you prepare for the study. Pray for discernment for yourself and for each member of the study group.
- Before each session, familiarize yourself with the content. Read the book chapter again.
- Choose the session elements you will use during the group session, including the specific discussion questions you plan to cover. Be prepared, however, to adjust the session as group members interact and as questions arise. Prepare carefully, but allow space for the Holy Spirit to move in and through the group members and through you as facilitator.

- If you plan to use video clips or music suggestions, obtain appropriate projection equipment and test it before the session in which you plan to use it.
- Prepare the space where the group will meet so that the space will enhance the learning process. Ideally, group members should be seated around a table or in a circle so that all can see one another. Movable chairs are best, because the group will often form pairs or small groups for discussion.
- Bring a supply of Bibles for those who forget to bring their own. It's fine, even helpful, to have a variety of translations.
- For most sessions you will also need an easel with paper and markers, a whiteboard and markers, or some other means of posting group questions and responses.

Shaping the Learning Environment

- Begin and end on time.
- Establish a welcoming space. Consider the room temperature, access to amenities, hospitality, outside noise, and privacy. Use a small cross or candle as a focal point for times of prayer.
- Create a climate of openness, encouraging group members to participate as they feel comfortable. As mentioned above, some participants may be uncomfortable or embarrassed about their experiences with money. Be on the lookout for signs of discomfort in those who may be silent, and encourage them to express their thoughts and feelings honestly. But assure the group members that passing on a question is always acceptable.

- Remember that some people will jump right in with answers and comments, while others will need time to process what is being discussed.
- If you notice that some group members seem never to be able to enter the conversation, ask them if they have thoughts to share. Give everyone a chance to talk, but keep the conversation moving. Moderate to prevent a few individuals from doing all the talking.
- Make use of the exercises that invite sharing in pairs. Those who are reluctant to speak out in a group setting may be more comfortable sharing one-on-one and reporting back to the group. This can often be an effective means of helping people grow more comfortable sharing in the larger setting. It also helps to avoid the dominance of the group by one or two participants (including you!).
- If no one answers at first during discussions, do not be afraid of silence. Help the group become comfortable with waiting. If no one responds, try reframing the language of the question. If no responses are forthcoming, venture an answer yourself and ask for comments.
- Model openness as you share with the group. Group members will follow your example. If you limit your sharing to a surface level, others will follow suit.
- Encourage multiple answers or responses before moving on to the next question.
- Ask, "Why?" or "Why do you believe that?" or "Can you say more about that?" to help continue a discussion and give it greater depth.
- Affirm others' responses with comments such as "Great" or "Thanks" or "Good insight"—especially if it's the first time someone has spoken during the group session.

- Monitor your own contributions. If you are doing most of the talking, back off so that you do not train the group to listen rather than speak up.
- Remember that you do not have all the answers. Your job is to keep the discussion going and encourage participation.

Managing the Session

- Honor the time schedule. If a session is running longer than expected, get consensus from the group before continuing beyond the agreed-upon ending time.
- When someone arrives late or must leave early, pause the session briefly to welcome them or bid them farewell. Changes in the makeup of the group change the dynamics of the discussion and need to be acknowledged. Every group member is important to the entire group.
- Involve group members in various aspects of the group session, such as saying prayers or reading the Scripture.
- As always in discussions that may involve personal sharing, confidentiality is essential. Group members should never pass along stories that have been shared in the group. Remind the group members at each session: confidentiality is crucial to the success of this study.

1.
We Don't Need
More Money;
We Need Wisdom

1.

We Don't Need More Money; We Need Wisdom

Planning the Session

Session Goals

As a result of conversations and activities connected with this session, group members should begin to:

- Reflect on biblical passages related to money and wisdom.
- Understand the meaning of both *money* and *wisdom*.
- Assess their relationships with money and wisdom.
- Explore John Wesley's teachings on the nature of money.

Biblical Foundation

Happy are those who find wisdom
   and those who gain understanding.
Her profit is better than silver,
   and her gain better than gold. (Proverbs 3:13-14)

Special Preparation

If group members are not familiar with one another, make nametags available.

Remember that there are more activities than most groups will have time to complete. As leader, you'll want to go over the session in advance and select or adapt the activities you think will work best for your group in the time allotted. Depending on which activities you select, you'll need to make some of the following special preparations.

- If possible in advance of the first session, ask participants to bring either a spiral-bound notebook or an electronic means of journaling, such as a tablet. Provide writing paper and pens for those who may need them. Also have a variety of Bibles available for those who do not bring one.
- Make sure all participants have a copy of the study book *Earn. Save. Give.* Invite them to read the Introduction and Chapter 1 in advance of the first session. You also should read this material.
- On a large sheet of paper or a board, print the following at the top: "Money is..."
- On another sheet, print: "Wisdom is . . ."
- Have available large sheets of blank paper or construction paper and colored markers for group activity.
- Depending on the size of your space, post some or all of the following Scripture references: 1 Kings 3:5-9; Proverbs 1:5-8; 2:6; 3:5, 7-10, 13-16; 4:7; 5:7; 8:23; 9:10; 11:15; 19:27; 23:19; Psalm 78:1-7; Matthew 6:33; Luke 16:8-9; 1 Timothy 6:10; James 1:5, 17.

Getting Started

Welcome

As participants arrive, welcome them to the study and invite them to make use of one of the available Bibles, if they did not bring one.

Opening Prayer

Gracious and Loving God, as we begin this study, open us to your presence and fill us—our time, our conversations, our reflections, our doubts, and our fears—with the joy of exploration and the wisdom of your love. We gather together in Jesus' name. Amen.

Opening Activities

When all participants have arrived, invite each person to introduce him- or herself by name and verbally complete one of the posted prompts ("Money is . . ." or "Wisdom is . . ."). When the circle is complete, invite general responses to each of the prompts and post them on the sheet or whiteboard. Participants may repeat their original response or add to it. Defining these terms provides a foundation and starting place for the study. Invite participants to add comments and new understandings to these definitions and lists during the weeks of the study.

If they have not already done so, invite group members to read the Introduction silently in the study book. Explore together:

- Author James A. Harnish suggests that money might be at the top of our lists if we could ask God for anything. Do you agree or disagree, and why?
- When you hear about the "wisdom of Solomon," what immediately comes to mind?
- Invite participants to read aloud 1 Kings 3:5-9 from at least three different translations. How do the various translations and paraphrases present Solomon's request in verse 9? (NRSV has "understanding mind"; NIV has "discerning heart"; CEB has "discerning mind"; *The Message* has "God-listening heart"; *Good News* has "wisdom.") Ask participants to describe the differences among these various phrases.
- Ask participants to read 1 Kings 3:11-14 aloud from various versions. Do you think the additional gifts to Solomon ("riches and honor" in NRSV; "wealth and fame" in CEB) are a blessing or curse? Why?
- Invite a volunteer to read the paragraph "Money Matters" in the Introduction. The author goes on to say that money matters for our souls and that wisdom is more valuable than money. Invite participants to respond to these ideas.

Learning Together

Video Study and Discussion

Pastor and author Jim Harnish introduces John Wesley—Christian theologian, evangelist, and founder of the Methodist movement—and Wesley's advice to "earn all you can, save all you can, give all you can." Harnish talks about the wisdom and challenges in that advice with three pastors: Justin Coleman, Judi Hoffman, and Erica Allen. Discuss:

- What are the biggest financial challenges faced by people in your community, church, and family? Give examples.
- How are those people coping with the challenges, and how can the church help?
- To the extent that you feel comfortable sharing, what are some examples of financial challenges, past or present, in your own life?
- What is your own experience regarding stewardship programs in churches?

Bible Study and Discussion

Throughout Chapter 1, the author examines biblical references to *wisdom*. Invite participants to form pairs. Each pair will take five minutes to read one of the following passages and share what it teaches about wisdom. It is unlikely that you will assign all the passages; assign at least the readings from Proverbs 2 and Matthew 7, and expand from there as your group size permits:

- Proverbs 1:5-8
- Proverbs 2:1-6
- Proverbs 3:5-10, 13-14
- Proverbs 9:7-10
- Matthew 6:19-21
- Matthew 6:25-33
- Matthew 7:24-29

- Matthew 24:45-51
- Philippians 4:12-13
- James 1:5-10

Invite the pairs back to the larger group to share insights from their conversations. If the group wants to add any new ideas or insights to the posted group "definition" of *wisdom*, invite participants to do so.

Book Study and Discussion

Money and Wisdom

In the opening section of Chapter 1, the author points to a commercial about "Stanley Johnson" and his relationship with money (consider viewing the brief video, which is available on YouTube; search for "Stanley Johnson commercial"). Harnish then shares some money-related concerns he encountered as a pastor.

In preparation for the conversation to follow about money and wisdom, ask participants to review Harnish's examples of money-related concerns ("As a pastor, I've seen..." through the five bullet points) and consider how those examples relate to their own lives and their experiences with money. After a time of silent reflection, invite responses to one or more of the following questions:

- What is your happiest memory in connection with money?
- What is your unhappiest memory in connection with money?

- Do you consider yourself a generous person? How do you define *generosity*?

These questions are designed to encourage participants to begin thinking about their relationships with money. Remember to be sensitive to the willingness of participants to share personal stories during this discussion. These and other questions related to one's relationship with money are adapted from *Money Autobiography*, a study tool created by Dan R. Dick.[1]

Wisdom Begins With God and Leads to Life

In Matthew 6:21, the author draws attention to the order of words: "Where your treasure is, there will your heart be also." He helps us see that we need wisdom to help us understand the true nature of both *treasure* and *heart*. This is followed by an exploration of the biblical understanding of wisdom lifted up throughout Proverbs, in the following sections of the chapter:

- Wisdom Begins With God
- Wisdom Is Passed on to the Next Generation
- Wisdom Is Better Than Wealth
- Wisdom Leads to Life

Form four small groups and ask each group to explore one of these sections of the chapter. Distribute large sheets of paper and markers, then invite each group to record their responses to the following and to choose a spokesperson:

- This is what the author means by this statement...
- We believe this statement is true in these ways...
- We have these questions about the information shared in this section...

After groups have had a chance to work, ask them to post their papers on the wall at intervals around your space. Have the spokesperson for each group report on the group's discussion. Then invite participants to share how this information and insight helps them to understand more completely the terms *wisdom*, *money*, *treasure*, and *heart*.

Wisdom From Wesley

The author shares insights from John Wesley's sermon "The Use of Money" as a foundation for understanding the importance of a right relationship with money and the pursuit of wisdom in its use.

- Invite a volunteer to read aloud Luke 16:1-13.
- Invite another volunteer to read aloud the author's commentary on Wesley's use of the passage (from "The story turns our expectations inside out" through the bullet points: "Gain all you can. Save all you can. Give all you can.").
- Ask participants to reflect on the relationship of the readings to their growing understanding of wisdom and money.

- Ask participants to share their responses, and invite them to post new insights on the various posted meanings of *money* and *wisdom*.

Wrapping Up

Closing Activity

Review your posted meanings of *money* and *wisdom*. Then split the group in half or form pairs and, based on the conversation during the session, invite the small groups to write meanings for each term. Have half the small groups write on *money* and half write on *wisdom*.

- Prepare two large, clean sheets of paper or whiteboard with the headings: "Money is…" and "Wisdom is…".
- Invite a representative of each group to post the new definitions.
- Invite responses and questions for consideration.
- *Note*: Record these definitions or save the newsprint. They will be revisited and refined in later sessions.
- Encourage participants to reflect on and journal about new understandings of and questions about *wisdom* and *money* as they read Chapter 2.
- How does wisdom relate to the way I earn money?
- How might wise management of our money benefit our congregation?

Closing Prayer

God of wisdom and love, fill us with your power as we leave this place, so that all we have shared and learned here helps us to be more faithful disciples. As your church in and for the world, we pray in the name of Jesus the Christ. Amen.

2.
Earn All
You Can

2.

Earn All You Can

Planning the Session

Session Goals

As a result of conversations and activities connected with this session, group members should begin to:

- Reflect on some biblical passages related to earning and using money.
- Understand the meaning of *calling, common sense,* and *expense* in relation to earning and managing money.
- Assess their relationships with the money they earn and the money they spend.
- Explore John Wesley's teachings on money and work.

Biblical Foundation

The wages of the righteous lead to life;
the earnings of the wicked lead to sin.
(Proverbs 10:16)

Special Preparation

If group members are not familiar with one another, make nametags available.

Remember that there are more activities than most groups will have time to complete. As leader, you'll want to go over the session in advance and select or adapt the activities you think will work best for your group in the time allotted. Depending on which activities you select, you'll need to make some of the following special preparations.

- Ask participants to bring their notebooks or electronic journals. Provide writing paper and pens for those who may need them. Also have a variety of Bibles available for those who do not bring one.
- Invite participants to read book Chapter 2 in advance of the session.
- Invite participants to reflect on and journal about the questions at the end of Session 1 in the Leader Guide. Ask them to consider one insight they might want to share with the group.
- Post the group's definitions of *money* and *wisdom* from the previous session.
- Post the following words[1] on a large sheet of paper or whiteboard:

power	security	hope	pleasure	love
identity	prestige	comfort	anxiety	gift
protection	need	value	burden	tool

- Have available blank paper or construction paper and markers or crayons.

- Have a large sheet of paper or whiteboard available for group activity.
- Locate a recording or the lyrics of "How Much Is Enough?" (The Fixx, 1991)[2] and a means to play it for the group.

Getting Started

Welcome

As participants arrive, welcome them to the study and invite them to make use of one of the available Bibles, if they did not bring one.

Opening Prayer

Calling God, we gather here to know you better, to learn ways for our lives to be more attuned to your will. Open us to your presence and assurance as we share our experiences and knowledge, our doubts and embarrassment. We humbly rely on you, Lord, and we pray in Jesus' name. Amen.

Opening Activities

When all participants have arrived, invite them to introduce themselves by name and to share a current or past source of income. (This will allow unemployed persons to participate without revealing they are not currently employed.) Be prepared for a variety of responses, from paying jobs outside the home to school loans to no current source of income. When the circle is complete, ask participants how it felt to share the source of their income. Ask them to record in their journals which of these posted words describe their feelings or attitudes about money. (They may choose more than one.)

power	security	hope	pleasure	love
identity	prestige	comfort	anxiety	gift
protection	need	value	burden	tool

If they have not already done so, invite group members to read silently the opening section of Chapter 2 through the section headed "The First Rule of Christian Wisdom" (ending with "...faithful followers of Jesus can earn all they can.").

- The author examines John Wesley's advice on the wise use of money. Together, review the group definitions of *wisdom* and *money* (from Session 1).
- Ask a volunteer to read aloud the two paragraphs that begin with "The first time I preached on Wesley's rules..." and ending with "...his money, and his faith." Ask participants how the businessman's sharing compares with sermons on money they have heard and their feelings related to preaching about money in the church.
- Invite group members to share understandings of wealth as both *prosperity* and *obstacle*.
- Play a recording of "How Much Is Enough?" by The Fixx (1991). Invite responses to the message of the song.
- Invite participants to share one new insight from their journals.

Learning Together

Video Study and Discussion

We meet entrepreneur and business mentor Michael Burcham. He discusses with Jim Harnish the power of money for good and describes ways in which he helps others discover where their great passion meets the world's great need. Discuss:

- Are you surprised by Wesley's advice to "earn all you can"? What do you think Wesley meant?
- When Jim says that Michael is channeling John Wesley, what do you think he means?
- If you feel comfortable sharing, give examples from your own life about earning in a healthy way and earning in an unhealthy way.
- Why do you think Wesley called money "God's excellent gift"? Do you agree? Why or why not?

Bible Study and Discussion

The chapter focuses on our approaches to earning and managing money. The author shares that John Wesley used a surprising passage, Luke 16:1-9, as the reading for his sermon, "The Use of Money." Harnish also lifts up selections from Proverbs and other biblical texts that illustrate the lessons offered by this story of the dishonest manager as well as other lessons about money management.

Invite participants to form five small groups. Each group will take time to read one of the following passages and discuss what it teaches about our relationship with money. Encourage the use of a variety of Bible translations and versions. Have each group choose a spokesperson.

- Luke 16:1-9 (the dishonest or shrewd manager)
- Matthew 19:24 (a camel through the eye of a needle)
- Proverbs 6:1-11 (the ant)
- Proverbs 31:13-24 (the wise woman)
- Luke 12:13-21 (the rich farmer)

Invite the groups back together to share insights and collective wisdom from their conversations. If the group wants to add any of the new ideas or insights to the posted group definitions of *wisdom* or *money*, invite the spokesperson to do so.

Book Study and Discussion

Gain All You Can by Honest Industry

Distribute blank paper and markers or crayons. Ask volunteers to read aloud from the study book the quotation from John Wesley's sermon that begins "Lose no time..." and the "Wisdom From the Proverbs" quotations. Invite participants to draw pictures of both *diligence* and *laziness*. They may draw stick figures in action, swatches of color, or whatever expresses the concepts.

You might encounter resistance to this or other "art" exercises. Assure participants that talent is not required here. This type of activity invites us to use different parts of our brains to examine our understanding of concepts. Invite skeptics to give it a try. Give some time for this activity and then invite persons to share their pictures (if they wish to do so).

Gain All You Can by Common Sense

Invite the group to stand. Place in the center or at the front of the room a symbol you will name as "common sense" (for example, a cross, candle, or Bible). Ask participants to stand close to or far from the symbol, based on their perception of their individual level of common sense.

As participants take their positions, invite them to explain how and why they chose to stand there. Self-perception always includes a range of responses that have to do with personality type and levels of emotional awareness as well as reasoning. You may be asked the purpose of the exercise. Placing ourselves in physical relation to a concept or goal helps us define it in a more visceral, experiential way than simply thinking or talking about it.

Gain All You Can Without Paying More for It Than It Is Worth

The author uses John Wesley's sermon "The Use of Money" as the entry point for a discussion of the various costs or expenses of our choices in relation to the money we earn. We generally think of *expense* as the opposite of *income*, an exchange in dollars and cents.

Harnish and Wesley invite us instead to count the cost of our material wealth in terms of our health, our soul, our neighbors, and our relationship with God. Choose one or more of the following:

- **Health**: Invite the group to discuss the difference between laziness and sabbath rest, and between *fulfilling a calling* and *overwork*. Encourage them to give examples from their own lives, including their lives in the faith community or congregation.
- **Soul**: Ask participants to share their understandings of the relationship between their calling and their work.
- **Neighbors**: Ask participants to make a list of all the "neighbors" who feel the impact of their work in "substance," "body," or "soul."
- **Relationship with God**: Invite participants to respond in silence to John Wesley's questions, "For what end do you undertake and follow your worldly business?" and "In what manner do you transact your worldly business?"

Wrapping Up

Closing Activity

Beginning to view our work and the money we earn or gain as God's *calling* on our lives may have revealed areas of vulnerability, even shame. This closing time will therefore focus on hope and healing.

Ask for volunteers to read aloud Matthew 11:28-29: "Come to me, all you who are struggling hard and carrying heavy loads, and I will give you rest. Put on my yoke, and learn from me. I'm gentle and humble. And you will find rest for yourselves." Ask participants how their understanding of this text is influenced by the work done during the session.

Closing Prayer

God of our calling and our riches, open our hearts to understand fully and share joyfully the lessons learned here about our relationship with the money we earn and use. As your church in and for the world, we pray in the name of Jesus the Christ. Amen.

3.
Save All
You Can

3.

Save All You Can

Planning the Session

Session Goals

As a result of conversations and activities connected with this session, group members should begin to:

- Reflect on biblical passages related to the concepts of stewardship and treasure.
- Understand the meaning of *steward* and *prudence* in relation to planning with and saving money.
- Assess their relationships with the money they save and the money they invest.
- Explore John Wesley's teachings on acquiring wealth and using it.

Biblical Foundation

> Riches gotten quickly will dwindle,
>   but those who acquire them gradually
>   become wealthy. (Proverbs 13:11)

"I, Wisdom, dwell with prudence;
I have found knowledge and discretion."
(Proverbs 8:12)

Special Preparation

If group members are not familiar with one another, make nametags available.

Remember that there are more activities than most groups will have time to complete. As leader, you'll want to go over the session in advance and select or adapt the activities you think will work best for your group in the time allotted. Depending on which activities you select, you'll need to make some of the following special preparations.

- Ask participants to bring their notebooks or electronic journals. Provide writing paper and pens for those who may need them. Also have a variety of Bibles available for those who do not bring one.
- Invite participants to read book Chapter 3 in advance of the session.
- Invite participants to reflect on and journal about the terms and concepts noted at the end of Session 2 in the Leader Guide. Ask them to consider one insight they might want to share with the group.
- Post the group definitions of *money* and *wisdom*.
- Have available blank paper or construction paper and markers or crayons.
- Have large sheets of paper or whiteboard available for group activity.

- There are three *Just Do It!* handouts in the appendix of this leader guide. Print enough copies of these handouts to distribute to each person at the end of the session.
- Bring the board game Monopoly to the session.
- Using Monopoly money (or other play money), prepare a stack of bills of equal denominations ($5, $10, or $20) that totals $1,000.
- Locate a recording or the lyrics of "Moving Forward?"[1] and a means to play it for the group.

Getting Started

Welcome

As participants arrive, welcome them to the study and invite them to make use of one of the available Bibles, if they did not bring one.

Opening Prayer

Gracious and loving God, as we share our reflections and learning in this time and place, help us to remember that you provide all the riches of our lives—material and spiritual. We pray that this time together leads us to more faithful stewardship of your gifts. Amen.

Opening Activities

When all participants have arrived, invite them to introduce themselves by name and ask them to share if they have prepared a will. (Assure the members that they don't have to answer about having prepared a will if they feel uncomfortable sharing such information.) When the circle is complete, ask participants what relevance that initial question regarding will preparation has to the material in Chapter 3.

- The author examines John Wesley's advice on the "second rule of Christian prudence"—saving all we can. Together, review the group definitions of *wisdom* and *money* (formed in Session 1 and perhaps refined in Session 2).
- Invite a volunteer to read aloud the first two paragraphs of book Chapter 3 ("Having earned...never too late to begin.").
- Ask participants to respond to the idea that saving "goes against the grain" of our culture.

Learning Together

Video Study and Discussion

Andrea and Bryan Burroughs introduce us to their young daughters and some ways in which the family saves and is learning to save. Bryan talks with Jim Harnish about how saving and managing financial resources is a part of their life with Christ. Discuss:

- In terms of money and saving, how would you say that Christians are "countercultural"? What does our culture say about saving? What does the church say?

- What role does money play in Andrea and Bryan's marriage relationship?
- Andrea and Bryan can't talk about saving without also talking about giving. Why do you think this is the case?

Bible Study and Discussion

In book Chapter 3, Harnish invites us to explore the stewardship of our financial assets. To help us understand the nature of stewardship and prudence, he revisits the story of the rich farmer, introduced in Chapter 2, and shares John Wesley's views on the subject.

Divide the group in half and distribute a large blank sheet and markers to each group. Ask each group to choose a spokesperson to report on their work. Ask one group to construct a definition of the word *steward* by using the passages below, their notes, and the section of the chapter headed "The Faithful Steward." Ask the other group to construct a definition of the word *prudence* by using the same passages, their notes, and the section of the chapter headed "The Prudent Manager." Encourage the use of a variety of Bible translations and versions, and have the groups select a spokesperson to report on their work.

- Proverbs 31:16 (the wise woman plants a vineyard)
- Mark 4:26-27 (the farmer who waits for seed to sprout)
- Matthew 25:14-30 (the parable of the talents / valuable coins)
- Luke 12:42-44 NRSV (the prudent manager)
- James 1:17 (every good and perfect gift)

- Luke 12:13-21 (the rich farmer; also see Session 2)
- Proverbs 8:12 (wisdom and prudence)
- Proverbs 13:11 (acquire riches gradually)
- Matthew 6:19-21 (earthly and heavenly treasures)
- Luke 14:28-30 (the foolish builder).

Invite a spokesperson from each group to post the definition their group constructed and to share insights from the group conversation.

Book Study and Discussion

Hoarding vs. Saving

On a large sheet of paper or section of board, draw a horizontal line with the word *Hoard* at one end and the word *Save* at the other end. Ask the participants to come forward and draw a hash mark and their name on the line, representing their relative position on the continuum from hoarding to saving. (An alternative approach to this exercise is to invite everyone to stand and place themselves on an imaginary continuum line across the room, with hoarding at one end and saving at the other.) Invite participants to share why they placed themselves where they did and how they feel about it.

You Need a Plan

The author explores a variety of approaches or plans for faithful stewardship in the ways we save and spend money. One of the approaches is the 10-10-80 plan. With Monopoly money (or other play money), using bills of equal denomination ($5, $10, or $20), count out three piles of money that together add up to $1,000: pile 1 = $100; pile 2 = $100; pile 3 = $800. Distribute blank sheets of paper or invite participants to record in their journals these numbers and how they compare with their own "plan" or distribution of income. Invite them to share responses to the exercise and any changes they might consider making in their distribution of funds.

Wrapping Up

Closing Activity

Though this chapter does offer practical advice for saving and planning, the essence of the message is spiritual.

- Read aloud the paragraph near the end of book Chapter 3 beginning "Wesley's rule to 'save all you can'. . . ", and invite participants to respond to the concept of saving all we can as a spiritual practice.
- Ask the group to consider how this faith community can help individuals be more faithful and prudent stewards.

Distribute the *Just Do It!* handouts, explaining that these are tools for thinking about and working on savings. Encourage participants to complete at least one step in the handouts during the coming week. Ask them, as they read Chapter 4, to reflect on any new understandings of wisdom, money, stewardship, prudence, and their relationship with money.

Closing Prayer

Loving God, you call us to use prudence and patience in managing our money. Help us to become more faithful stewards of all the gifts you give—of life, of love, of joy—so that those who follow us will know your love through us. We are your church, your witness in and for the world, and so we pray in the name of Jesus the Christ. Amen.

4.
Give All
You Can

4.

Give All You Can

Planning the Session

Session Goals

As a result of conversations and activities connected with this session, group members should begin to:

- Reflect on biblical passages related to the concepts of giving and generosity.
- Understand the meaning of *stewardship*, *salvation*, and *sacrifice* in relation to money and other assets.
- Assess their relationships with the money they give and the money they share.
- Explore John Wesley's teachings on giving all we can.

Biblical Foundation

> Generous persons will prosper;
> those who refresh others will themselves be
> refreshed. (Proverbs 11:25)

Special Preparation

If group members are not familiar with one another, make nametags available.

Remember that there are more activities than most groups will have time to complete. As leader, you'll want to go over the session in advance and select or adapt the activities you think will work best for your group in the time allotted. Depending on which activities you select, you'll need to make some of the following special preparations.

- Ask participants to bring their notebooks or electronic journals. Provide writing paper and pens for those who may need them. Also have a variety of Bibles available for those who do not bring one.
- Invite participants to read book Chapter 4 in advance of the session.
- Invite participants to reflect on and journal about the terms and concepts that are presented in Session 3. Ask them to consider one insight they might want to share with the group.
- Post the group's definitions of *money* and *wisdom*.
- Provide a large jar or bowl (or an unlined offering plate) and a large quantity of buttons or marbles or any small pieces that will make noise when they are dropped into the receptacle.
- Have available blank paper or construction paper and markers or crayons.
- Have large sheets of paper or whiteboard available for group activity.

- View the movie *Millions* (2004), a story of the ways we relate to money and of extravagant generosity. Prepare a clip to share with the group. The scene with Damian and his mother by the railroad tracks illustrates the true meaning of generosity.

Getting Started

Welcome

As participants arrive, welcome them to the study and invite them to make use of one of the available Bibles, if they did not bring one.

Opening Prayer

Generous and giving God, we are yours. We pray that this time of sharing and learning moves us to more extravagant generosity and more joy-filled living and giving. In the name of Jesus the Christ, we pray. Amen.

Opening Activities

When all participants have arrived, invite them to introduce themselves by name and to share the greatest gift they have ever given or received.

The author explores John Wesley's challenge to give all we can. Together, review the group's definitions of *wisdom* and *money*. Ask participants to comment on the relationship between wisdom and giving.

- Invite participants who wish to do so to share the results of their "Just Do It!" worksheets and any plans they have made to "move forward" in their saving.
- Encourage participants to share one new insight from their journals.

Learning Together

Video Study and Discussion

We see Madeline Walls at her church, reflecting on a life of giving—by serving the homeless, teaching young people to read, digging up weeds, parking cars, tithing. She and Jim Harnish talk about how she grew up in a family that gave and how she seeks to pass along her blessings to others. Discuss:

- Madeline's giving includes weeding and parking cars! Comment on what this shows about Madeline and what we can learn from it.
- Discuss the role of Madeline's family in her attitudes and practices of giving.
- Wesley described giving as the "farther end" of earning and saving. What do you think he meant? Discuss the relationship among earning, saving, and giving, in terms of both finances and faith.

Bible Study and Discussion

In book Chapter 4, the author shares the stories of three "witnesses" who confirm the wisdom of Wesley's third rule for the use of money. In the book-study section below, we will explore the biblical stories of Zacchaeus and the unnamed widow. In this Bible-study section, we will focus on a text related to the first witness, Big Daddy from Tennessee Williams's play, "Cat on a Hot Tin Roof."

- Ask for volunteers to read aloud, from a variety of Bibles, 1 Timothy 6:17-19. Be sure to include the King James Version as one of the translations. Its language for verse 18 is very different from other common translations ("distribute" and "communicate" rather than "be generous" and "share"). Invite initial responses to the passage and the various versions.

- Ask a volunteer to read aloud the section of the book under the heading "Charity or Stewardship?" As the section is being read, post at the top of a large sheet of paper or whiteboard the terms *Charity* and *Stewardship* and the characteristics of each.

- Invite the group members to give examples that illustrate each concept as they are defined in the book and in the passage from First Timothy. Record these under the headings, as they are shared. Some examples are shown on the next page.

Charity	Stewardship
happens in a moment	takes a lifetime
given out of abundance	changes financial priorities
makes a difference for the receiver	makes a difference in the giver
response to immediate need	discipline that leads to spiritual maturity

As you review the two lists, invite participants to share whether they feel that they engage in charity or stewardship and why. Be prepared for the "both/and" response: that a life of stewardship often results in acts of charity.

Book Study and Discussion

Salvation and Zacchaeus

Harnish states that Zacchaeus "experienced salvation" through his willingness to be humble and foolish in that tree and in his extravagant response to Jesus' invitation. Note that *salvation* is not a word commonly used in Western culture.

- Invite a volunteer to read the story of Zacchaeus from the Bible (Luke 19:1-10).
- Now read for the group the author's definition of *salvation* ("Zacchaeus's witness underscores...in the lives of others.") and his statement that salvation is not earned by giving ("Zacchaeus did not earn...energized by giving.").

Invite participants to share their responses to these statements about salvation and to offer definitions that may differ from the author's.

- Divide into pairs and ask the participants to share their experiences of salvation or their hopes for salvation.
- Re-form the group and invite participants to share any new understandings gained about salvation.

Sacrifice and the Widow

- The author uses the parable known as "The Widow's Mite" to introduce a discussion of giving.
- Position a large jar or bowl at the front of the room. Place the supply of marbles or buttons at the other end of the room, reserving one of the smallest pieces from the pile.
- Have participants come one at a time to take a handful of marbles or buttons, as many as they like, until all but the one you have held in reserve are distributed. If you run out before everyone in the group has taken something, quietly give the one small piece to someone who has none. If not, you will use the one small piece.
- Have the group members count the number of items they have taken. List the names and amounts on a large sheet of paper or whiteboard.
- Invite each person to go to the front of the room and drop, not place, marbles or buttons into the jar or bowl (so that they make noise). The one with the most goes first, and the one with the single piece goes last.

- Invite responses to the exercise. How did it feel to drop items in the jar in front of everyone? Was it fun to make noise with lots of marbles (or buttons)? How did it feel to be the last person to go?
- Ask for volunteers to read the account of the widow's offering in Mark 12:41-44 and Luke 21:1-4.
- Ask the group to discuss the impact of giving our offerings in a way where the amount is easily discernible. Would it change our level of giving? Why?

The Nature of Sacrifice

- As with the understanding of *calling* explored in book Chapter 2, Harnish invites readers to an expanded understanding of *sacrifice* as a joyful, positive aspect of stewardship.
- Divide into three groups. Invite the groups to review the section of the text headed "Giving for the Joy of It." Ask each group to consider this question: What is the difference between joyful sacrifice and sacrifice as an obligation? Ask them to illustrate their answer in the form of a story, poem, song, or picture. Have available blank paper and markers and construction paper. Ask the groups to choose a spokesperson to report on their work.
- Invite the groups back together to share their responses and illustrations.

Wrapping Up

Closing Activity

In the final book chapter, the author invites us to see the larger context of our relationship with money and our relationship with God. It is critical that participants leave the study with a commitment to carry out any plans they have made regarding the financial stewardship of their earning, saving, and giving.

- If you have prepared a clip from *Millions*, show it now and invite participants to respond to the ideas it raises about generosity.
- Invite responses to the following questions[1] (this can also be done in pairs):
  - How has your relationship with God been influenced by your relationship with money?
  - How has your relationship with money been influenced by your relationship with God?
  - If you could ask God for anything, what would it be?

- Ask participants willing to do so to share plans they have made in regard to earning, saving, and giving.

- Ask the group how this faith community can help individuals connect their relationship with money to their relationship with God and one another.

Closing Prayer

Generous and giving God, we have explored, shared, learned, and questioned together. Thank you. Help us to take the lessons from this time into our lives so that people can see your love alive in us. Open us to your presence and power and to one another as we seek to earn, save, and give—to love—in grateful response to your extravagant generosity. In Christ's name we pray. Amen.

Appendix

Just Do It!
Plan for Saving
All I Can

Face the Facts
Financial Inventory

Using figures from the last full calendar year or the last twelve months, enter rounded totals for your income and for your expenses in the areas of giving, saving, and living. Subtract the total for expenses in all three areas from the total income and record the answer in the final row.

Annual Income	$
Giving Include church and other charitable giving	$
Saving Include contributions to retirement plans, savings accounts.	$
Living Include rent/mortgage, utilities (heat, water, phone, Internet), clothing, food, cable, work/school (necessary transportation, meals, tuition), debt service (loan payment, credit card interest, etc.)	$
Annual Expense **(Giving + Saving + Living)**	$
The Facts to Face **(Annual income minus expenses)**	$

Learn From Others:
Estate Distribution Planning

List the beneficiaries of your long-term investments (retirement planning, trusts, life insurance, wills). If you have not assigned beneficiaries or have no long-term investments, discuss and record your plans for prudent investment for the future.

Long-Term Planning	Beneficiary	Amount
Retirement Accounts		$
Trusts		$
Life Insurance		$
Will		$
Other		$
Plans		$

Simplify Spending:
Do Plastic Surgery

List all credit cards and the outstanding balance on each. Cut up all of your credit cards that have zero balances (it is not necessary to close the accounts).

Card Name	Balance Due	Date Destroyed
	$	
	$	
	$	
	$	
	$	
	$	
	$	
	$	
	$	
	$	
	$	
	$	
	$	
	$	
	$	
	$	
	$	
	$	
	$	

Notes

Session 1. We Don't Need More Money; We Need Wisdom
1. From *Money Autobiography*, created by the Rev. Dan R. Dick, available at http://doroteos2.com/2015/02/11/money-autobiography/. Questions used by permission.

Session 2. Earn All You Can
1. From *Money Autobiography*, http://doroteos2.com/2015/02/11/money-autobiography/
2. Find the lyrics for "How Much Is Enough?" here: http://www.metrolyrics.com/how-much-is-enough-lyrics-the-fixx.html. Hear an MP3 sample and download the recording here: http://www.amazon.com/How-Much-Is-Enough/dp/B000WOQY0O.

Session 3. Save All You Can
1. Find the lyrics for "Moving Forward?" here: http://www.metrolyrics.com/moving-forward-lyrics-hoobastank.html. Hear an MP3 sample and download the recording here: http://www.amazon.co.uk/gp/product/B001KSRNCO/ref=dm_ws_ap_tlw_trk63.

Session 4. Give All You Can
1. Questions are from *Money Autobiography*, http://doroteos.com/2015/02/11/money-autobiography/.